MAKING YOUR OWN
PAPIER MÂCHÉ

MELANIE WILLIAMS

NH
NEW
HOLLAND

First published in the UK in 1995 by
New Holland (Publishers) Ltd
Chapel House, 24 Nutford Place,
London W1H 6DQ

ISBN 1 85368 302 7

Editor Coral Walker
Art director Jane Forster
Design assistant Sarah Willis
Photographer Shona Wood
Illustrator Terry Evans
Calligrapher David Harris

Phototypeset by Ace Filmsetting Ltd, Frome, Somerset
Originated by HBM Print Pte Ltd, Singapore
Printed and bound in Singapore by Kyodo Printing
Co (Pte) Ltd

Contents

Introduction

Papier mâché is an ancient craft of international interest. Wherever in the world you discover papier mâché, you will find different approaches are employed in the scale, decoration and function of the piece. This results in a refreshingly wide range of images which can be taken happily on board when embarking on the craft itself.

This craft technique demands very little in the way of expensive materials or equipment; you are likely to find a number of the basic requirements around your own home, for example, newspaper, flour, white emulsion paint and glue.

In the following chapters I have tried to cover a selection of ideas, techniques and levels of skill to suit everyone. All the projects are colourful, original, stylish and are decorated using a variety of techniques and surface finishes.

Many of the projects are very simple and are aimed at people who may be embarking on papier mâché for the first time or for those working with children. The decorative egg cups on page 32, the bowl on page 66, bird mobile on page 44 and the pen holders on page 72 are all ideal beginners' projects.

Also included in the book are a number of

items to make which demand a little more concentration and time, such as the carriage clock (page 83), Hawaiian doll (page 80), key cabinet (page 58) and bouquet (page 20).

The projects involve both pulp and strip papier mâché, working with chicken wire, and incorporating string, beads and feathers to form relief patterns and decoration. There are a number of different decorative paint techniques too, such as spattering, sponging, distressing and simple freehand painting.

To help you become familiar with the basic materials and equipment necessary to achieve success when working with papier mâché, I have included a chapter 'How to begin' which clearly takes you through what essentials you will need and the basic techniques of papier mâché. Each project lists the materials necessary to make the item, but you can vary the colours and shapes to create something more original and in your own style.

Whatever projects you choose to try, I am sure you will have lots of fun and pleasure making them. And remember, however experienced or inexperienced you are, this craft offers you great potential for instant success, so turn the pages and get started.

Chapter 1
How to begin

There are two basic ways of using papier mâché: strip and pulp. **Strip** involves different sized pieces of paper, depending on the scale of the project on which you are working, combined with a flour and water based paste. The **pulp** method involves mixing small pieces of paper with a water and PVA solution until it becomes sodden and pulpy. Alternatively you can put the mixture into a food blender and whizz it to obtain a paper mush.

Paste

In this book we have used flour and water paste, but there are a number of alternatives that can be used in papier mâché. You can use non-fungicidal wallpaper pastes, which have full directions on the packet. Another possibility is well-diluted PVA medium.

Flour and water paste is, without doubt, the cheapest and least harmful mixture. To prepare the flour and water paste add a small amount of cold water to approximately 50–80 g (2–3 oz) of plain sieved white flour in a mixing bowl. Mix this together using a fork to form a paste. Gradually add enough water until you obtain a mixture with the consistency of a thick batter.

Paper

Throughout, we have used newspaper. This is torn – never cut – into strips which will result in a softer, neater finish. To obtain neat long strips, tear the paper along the grain. You can work this out for yourself because the paper will not tear easily the other way. The size of the pieces you need to prepare will be dictated by the scale of the project.

Basic techniques

Cardboard structures: This is one of the simplest ways of building up papier mâché items. One or several shapes are drawn or traced (using a template, see page 17) on to cardboard. Depending on the item, you can use medium weight cardboard, such as cereal packets or thick, corrugated cardboard or mounting board. The shape is then cut out using scissors or a craft knife. (A craft knife should be used in conjunction with a steel ruler and cutting mat.) Some of the projects will involve several cardboard pieces being stuck together to form, for example, a box or little house.

Use masking tape to secure the joins, as this will be covered later. When the cardboard structure is complete, several layers of papier mâché are applied to neatly cover and disguise all the joins and edges. In the case of the simple pieces, like the Christmas decorations (page 30), papier mâché is applied directly to the shape.

> **Note:** To make really secure joints on cardboard items, run a piece of masking tape along the whole length of the join before you add the papier mâché. Then tape a few small strips across the join.

This little house, kennel and the cheerful flowers are all made from medium weight cardboard. Recycle cereal packets or other packaging.

Moulds: You can basically take a papier mâché mould from any shape which does not absorb moisture, ie bowls, vases, plates, shells, balloons and eggs. Before applying the strips and paste you must prepare the surface of the mould. With the exception of balloons, the surfaces must be coated first with a layer of petroleum jelly then with water-soaked strips of paper. This prevents paste coming into contact with the mould and making it difficult to remove later.

Three to four layers of papier mâché strips need to be applied to the mould, depending on how thick you want your object. Avoid air bubbles, lumps and folds by using your fingers to smooth down the strips, smearing paste out on either side of the paper. Wipe off any excess paste with your fingers. The covered mould should then be left in a warm place to dry, an airing cupboard is

ideal. Avoid direct heat as this can cause warping and an unsatisfactory result. Papier mâché, if not dried properly, is vulnerable to mildew, so the drying step is important. Once fully dry, the mould can be removed gently. Sometimes, particularly stubborn shapes can be difficult to prise off the mould. If this is the case, use a sharp craft knife to make a slit in the papier mâché. Ease this slit apart, and the papier mâché should come away. Glue the slit together neatly; it will be covered by more layers of papier mâché later.

Chicken wire: Awkward shapes, especially figures, are moulded around a wire model or armature. Choose the smallest gauge of chicken wire as this is easier to manipulate into the required shape. You may want to wear gloves of some sort to protect your hands from the sometimes sharp wire. The wire can be cut using either an old pair of scissors or wirecutters. To join up bits of wire, simply bend them over one another.

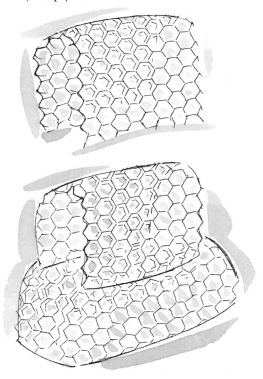

On wire models, the body, head and limbs are made separately. These pieces are then pushed together and the wire is intertwined. For movable joints, build each piece with papier mâché and when dry, sew together.

Straight wire: This type of wire is very useful when working with papier mâché. It can be purchased from gardening or DIY shops in a number of different thicknesses.

Cut these wires using pliers or wirecutters. Wire is used in a number of projects in this book, including flowers and animals. It is bent into shape, for example, a petal, then covered with a couple of layers of papier mâché strips.

Pulping paper: This is frequently used for creating jewellery or small details like little ball feet for boxes. It can also be added to surfaces to create relief detail or moulded around a knitting needle to make beads.

To prepare the paper pulp, place small pieces of paper in a water and PVA mixture until they become mushy. Mix the pulp together with a fork or place in a food blender to obtain a fine mush.

To mould the paper pulp into shapes, you must take a small handful and squeeze out the mixture. Leave the shapes to dry thoroughly before decorating.

Relief detail: Some of the projects may suggest gluing string or card shapes to the structure before covering it in papier mâché.

This creates a relief pattern that will clearly show up as a design once you have added the papier mâché layers. The relief can be picked out in a contrasting colour when you are painting the item, or rubbed with gilt wax for a sparkling flourish.

Attractive relief designs can be built up using simple household string or twine. Create random squiggles, or glue the twine into a formal pattern, as shown here.

Feet, handles and other details:

Appendages, such as feet, can be added to the item before the final stage of papier mâché. Feet can be made from small tubes of cardboard (see page 74) or scrunched up balls of paper covered in papier mâché strips (page 88). Secure the feet to the item using masking tape or, in the case of ball feet, a blob of glue and a dressmaker's pin.

Handles can be formed in the same way, or by using straight wire, which is pushed into the object and bent into shape.

Wire handles need to be covered in several layers of papier mâché, blending and securing the points of entry with more papier mâché strips.

Sanding and priming

Once you are happy with the shape or structure you have created and the papier mâché is completely dry, the next step is to gently smooth the surface down with fine grade sandpaper. You may need to use tiny pieces of sandpaper to reach difficult corners. Brush away the excess paper dust from the surface and apply a layer of white matt emulsion paint over the whole surface of the object.

Painting and decorating

Once the surface has been primed and is completely dry it is ready to be decorated in the desired way. There are a wide range of finishes illustrated in this book. You may like to use a light pencil to draw an intricate or detailed design on to the surface, before you apply the paint. We have used water-based poster paints throughout this book as they seem to be the most satisfactory when working on this surface. However gouache or water colours would be equally suitable. You may like to layer various bright colours, and once they are fully dry, sand the surface down with fine sandpaper to allow the different colours to show through. This is known as **distressing**.

Be sure to paint a coat of white emulsion paint between each layer of colour, and allow each coat of paint to dry fully before applying the next.

This 'distressed' Christmas heart has first been painted blue, then white, then finished with a wash of yellowy-green. By lightly sanding the piece, the blue undercoat shows through in places.

A natural sponge lightly dipped in paint can also create an interesting effect. Apply one colour with the sponge randomly over the object.

Another paint technique you may like to use is **spattering**. This is a simple way of obtaining a grainy, three-dimensional effect. Use a square ended brush or old toothbrush coated in quite watery but strong coloured paint. Hold the brush approximately 15 cm (6 in) away from the surface and use your forefinger or a knife to pull back the bristles, resulting in the spattering of paint. Using a variety of colours makes this technique more interesting and effective.

> *Note: Always make sure that each layer of paint dries completely before applying the next. This also applies to adding in painted features, like eyes.*

Allow this painted layer to dry before applying another colour with the sponge, overlapping the first.

Spattering takes minutes, yet the results are most effective, especially when used to create a textured finish, such as on this animal's coat.

A thick paint and a more watery wash has been applied to the basic cat to create an interesting effect before the other decoration is added.

Decorating with paper

There are a number of beautiful decorative papers available which make fabulous and abstract designs. This technique works especially well on large, simple pieces such as bowls, plates or vases. Use watered down PVA medium to adhere the paper to the surface. Teasing, rather than cutting with scissors, looks attractive, although it depends what effect you want to achieve. The lighter the weight of the paper, the easier it is to use, and the more smoothly it will lie on the surface.

Varnishing

Once you have decorated your creation satisfactorily, and it is fully dry, you will need to coat the surface both on top and underneath with varnish. In some cases, you may need two coats. We have suggested using a wood polyurethane varnish in either a matt or gloss finish, or you can mix the two and obtain a satin finish. You will need white spirit to clean the brush you use.

This final process both protects the painted surface, and also the papier mâché beneath. However, although the papier mâché is coated in varnish, it is not fully water proof and must be kept away from moisture.

Other decorative materials

A number of other materials will be required when finishing many of the projects in this book. These include beads, feathers, metallic powders, gilt wax or gold rubbing paste, jewellery fittings, string, sequins and magnets.

Adhesives

Glue is an essential requirement in most of the projects in this book. We suggest using white PVA medium which is both waterbased and dries clear. Most of the time the glue alone will be strong enough to secure fixtures and long dress pins can assist in holding feet and handles into position as extra security. All-purpose clear glue can also be used to stick some items.

> *Note:* Coloured tissue paper looks particularly pretty on papier mâché items. Stick the tissue in a pleasing pattern, overlapping some pieces, to create a wonderful translucent effect.

Templates and patterns

Some items in this book have templates or patterns for you to use as a guide. This is necessary for more complicated pieces, such as the key cabinet on page 58 as well as being especially helpful if you are not a very confident artist. If the instructions show a template, this can be traced directly and transferred on to the cardboard or whatever. Patterns shown smaller must be scaled up.

Scaling up: You can use a photocopier with an enlarger facility; this is probably the easiest way. Alternatively, you can scale up with a simple grid.

Trace the original design on to tracing paper. Draw a grid over the tracing. On another piece of paper, draw a larger grid containing the same number of squares.

Copy the original picture on to the larger grid, matching square for square.

You are now ready to transfer the larger design on to the cardboard or other material.

Chapter 2
Decorations

Flower bouquet

This project illustrates an effective way of capturing the vibrant yet delicate form of a bouquet of flowers. We chose to recreate anemones by using small strip papier mâché and wire combined with effective paint finishes and adding realistic detail. This technique can be adapted to make a number of other varieties.

Although these flowers look stunning displayed in an existing vase you may have, you could always create a vase using papier mâché to a specific design or colour. See page 62 for details of how to make a papier mâché vase.

REQUIREMENTS
Wire
Flour and water paste
Newspaper strips
Large needle
Paper scraps
PVA glue
Fine grade sandpaper
White emulsion paint
Poster paints
Varnish

1 Using wirecutters or a pair of old scissors, cut the wire into pieces between 5–7 cm (2–3 in) long. You will need six pieces of wire for each flower, so if you wish to make five flowers, cut 30 pieces.

Note: *When drying out all the papier mâché, you may like to speed up the process by placing all the parts on a baking tray and putting them in a cool oven with the door slightly open. Watch them carefully until they are dry.*

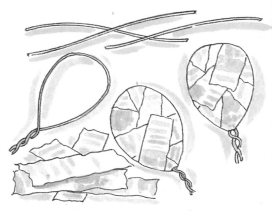

2 Bend the lengths of wire into loops, twisting the ends to secure them. Proceed to wrap strips of paper and paste around all the petal shapes. You will need to use two layers, otherwise the petals will lose their delicacy. Leave all the petals in a warm place to dry.

3 To make the centre part of the flower, roll up a piece of paper into a ball, the size of a cherry tomato. Neaten up the surface by wrapping a few layers of papier mâché around it. Make as many balls as necessary and leave them in a warm place to dry.

4 Cut the wire into 15–20 cm (6–8 in) lengths for the stems. Using a large needle, pierce a hole into each papier mâché ball, add a blob of glue and insert the stem wire. Proceed to wrap a number of layers of papier mâché strips up and down the stem securing the ball to the stem as you go. Leave the half completed flowers in a warm place to dry.

Although contemporary and stylized, this bunch of papier mâché anemones looks perfectly at home in a country cottage when displayed in a simple jug.

paper and paste. It can be quite fiddly, but if you use thinner strips and patience, the leaves should be successful. Make as many leaves as you require and leave them in a warm place to dry.

7 Once all the flowers and leaves are fully dry, gently smooth down any lumps or bumps, using fine sandpaper. Prime all the smooth flowers and leaves with white emulsion paint.

8 Proceed to paint all the stems in a shade of green first. Now paint the petals. Using either your thumb or fine sandpaper rub the surface of the petals (if you choose to rub with your thumb, the paint must still be wet). Paint the middles of the flowers in a black/brown colour. Add detail around the base of the petals by applying fine black-brown lines coming away from the centre. You may also like to spatter the completed flowerheads with either a very dark or light colour, (they will show up better). Paint the leaves in a shade of green, rub or spatter in the same way as you did with the petals.

9 Once you are happy with the way you have decorated your flowers and leaves, coat them in a gloss varnish.

5 Now take all the petal shapes and divide them into sets of six equal sizes. Neaten the blunt wire at the base of the petals by snipping it off. Using the large needle, make six equidistant holes in the ball, or centre part, of each flower. Apply a large blob of glue into each hole and proceed to insert the petals.

Note: Use very small, thin pieces of paper when following this project. By doing this you will be more successful at achieving the delicate floral details.

Variations
We chose to illustrate anemones in this project because they are a strong, bold flower of vibrant colour. This will enable you to produce a more convincing replica. Flimsy, tissue-like flowers are less suitable to recreate in this medium. Instead try tulips, sunflowers, pansies and large daisies.

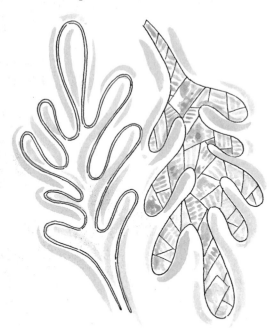

6 To make the leaves, cut a length of wire, approximately 38 cm (15 in), for each leaf. Bend the wire into an anemone leaf shape, as shown, starting at one end of the wire and eventually joining up with the other end. The leaf shape should be flat. Now proceed to cover the whole shape in slim strips of

Duet of sheep

This charming duet of ceramic-like sheep incorporate a basic fine gauge chicken wire frame, which is then covered in narrow strips of papier mâché. Once the shape is built up, the sheep is decorated using a variety of paint techniques.

By spattering and sanding, an interesting antique effect is created; this combined with the fine detailed border around the bottom successfully evokes memories of original ceramic animal figurines and ornaments from days gone by.

Resembling a pair of Staffordshire pottery figurines, these delightful sheep will sit contentedly on any shelf or mantelpiece. The models are formed around simple wire frames, which can be slightly modified to make the creatures look up or down.

REQUIREMENTS
Small gauge chicken wire
Flour and water paste
Newspaper strips
Cardboard
Masking tape
Pins
All-purpose glue
Fine grade sandpaper
White matt emulsion paint
Paint to decorate
Varnish

1 Using either an old pair of scissors or wirecutters, cut out four pieces of chicken wire; two pieces measuring approximately 18 x 13 cm (7 x 5 in), and the other two measuring approximately 13 x 15 cm (5 x 6 in). The larger pieces will form the base and the other two will form the sheep bodies.

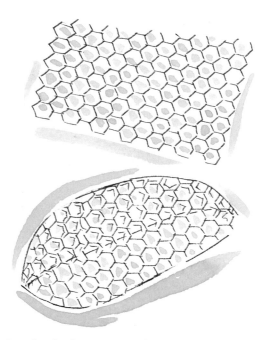

4 Once you have formed the basic wire shapes, which should be as similar to each other as possible, cover the shapes in two to three layers of papier mâché, making sure you cover under the bases as well. Leave the shapes to dry in a warm place.

2 Take the base pieces of wire and bend any protruding bits under to make a neat edge along each long side. Squeeze the wire mesh together at each end so that it takes the form of a boat hull upside down.

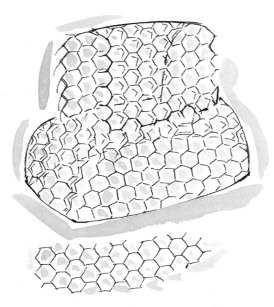

5 Using the scissors or wirecutters, cut out two more pieces of the wire mesh measuring approximately 5 x 6.5 cm (2 x 2½ in). These will form the sheeps' heads. Bend the wire into tube shapes and tuck the protruding wires in to close one end; use the spikes of wire at the other end to attach the head to the body.

6 Now apply two or three more layers of papier mâché to the sheep models. Keep the surface as smooth and lump free as possible, using your fingers to push out any bumps or bubbles. Leave the sheep in a warm place and allow to dry.

3 Now take the other two pieces of wire and bend them gently in half, tucking in the protruding wire spikes at each end. Attach these 'sheep bodies' to their bases by tucking and folding the wire spikes into the mesh, as shown.

10 Paint the bodies of the sheep in an off-white colour and when dry, rub the surface down gently as before. To achieve a fleecy look to the woolly coats, spatter dark brown paint on to the off-white. (Spattering is explained more fully on page 16.) This will create an interesting texture. Paint the head and ears in dark brown or black and once dry add little eyes in white paint.

7 To make the ears, draw four oval ear shapes on to a piece of card. Cut these out. Attach a pin to each ear with a small piece of tape; the pins will hold the ears on to the sheep's head. Apply a blob of glue to the base of each ear and push the pin into the head. Apply a few thin strips of paper and paste around the ears so that they blend in with the rest of the body. Leave them in a warm place to dry.

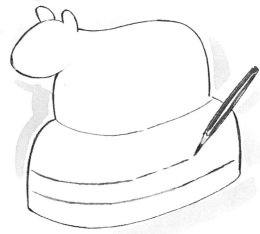

11 Using a fine pencil, lightly mark out a repeating pattern around the border of the hillocks. Fill in your design with contrasting colours of paint. Finally, coat the duet of sheep in matt or gloss varnish.

8 Smooth down the surface of the sheep with sandpaper and apply one coat of white emulsion paint. When the paint is dry, mark out the border lines around the base of the hillocks with a pencil.
9 Paint the hillocks, applying the colour so that you neatly avoid the border. When thoroughly dry, rub the surface gently with sandpaper, to achieve a worn, antique look.

> **Note:** Once you have painted the hillocks, the unpainted border left around the base may look messy and have an uneven edge. If so, place two strips of masking tape along the top and bottom of the border and fill it in with the white emulsion paint, or possibly another colour. Once dry, remove the masking tape carefully to reveal neat, straight edges.

Fruit salad

This mouth-watering selection of papier mâché fruit is created by simply covering balls of screwed up newspaper with strips of papier mâché then finishing with some effective paint techniques. These include spattering, sanding and highlighting. To create a successful fruit bowl it is important to recreate a variety of shapes and colours, as we have done here, for example a pineapple, grapes and bananas.

REQUIREMENTS
Paper scraps
Masking tape
Flour and water paste
Newspaper strips
PVA glue
Wire
Green paper
Green florists' wire
Large needle
Cardboard
Fine grade sandpaper
White matt emulsion paint
Poster paints
Gloss varnish

Round fruits

To create round shaped fruits such as a pineapple, pear, strawberries, apples and grapes, the same basic technique is used, although the scale is different for each one.

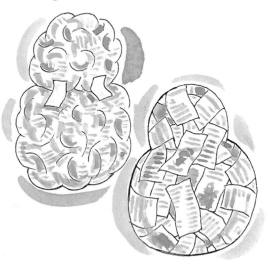

1 Begin by screwing up a piece of paper into a ball. To make a **pear**, for example, screw up a piece of paper about A4 in size, then screw up another smaller piece of paper.

Tape the two balls together to create a rough pear shape. Use the same screwed up paper technique with the other rounded fruits. (Make each grape separately, instructions explaining how to join them up into a bunch is provided in step 4.)

2 Proceed to wrap the basic newspaper shape with three to four layers of papier mâché, trying to keep the surface as smooth and lump free as possible. Avoid getting your work too wet and soggy. Once you are happy with the shape, leave it in a warm place to dry out.

3 Using fine grade sandpaper, smooth down the surface of the fruit shapes, putting each one aside ready for painting.

4 To make the bunch of **grapes** you will need to join the shapes together before painting them. Using PVA glue, begin to join the grapes together one by one, allowing the glue to dry between every couple of grapes, so that the growing bunch can support the additional grapes. Once the bunch is ready, cut two or three lengths of wire, approximately 7–10 cm (3–4 in) long. Twist the wire around a pencil to form a spiral. Push the wire tendrils into the top of the bunch of grapes, securing them in place with a blob of glue.

This striking mock fruit makes a delightful decoration for a coffee table. Display the pieces on a wooden platter, or even a papier mâché one! Don't worry about making up the fruit all in one go; add to your collection over time.

6 You may need to sand the fruits a little more, but when you are happy with them, apply a coat of matt white emulsion paint to them all.

7 Mix up the colours you require to achieve a realistic finish. Start with a base coat, for example a light acid green for the pear and a dull orange for the pineapple. Then proceed to add detail to the surface to achieve a more realistic and convincing replica of the fruit. You could gently sand the surface to distress it and give a rough appearance.

5 To complete the **pineapple** you need to add a number of leaves to the top. Cut approximately 8–10 lengths of wire between 12–25 cm (5–10 in) – you want the leaves to be all different sizes. Bend the pieces of wire in half, to form a pineapple leaf shape. Wrap the leaves with two or three layers of papier mâché strips and leave them in a warm place to dry. Once dry, gently sand them smooth. Using the end of a pair of scissors, make a hole in the top of the pineapple.

8 The **strawberry** hulls are only added once the fruits have been painted. To make the hulls, tear green paper into 2.5 cm (1 in) long strips. Snip a piece of florists' wire about 2 cm (¾ in) long for each strawberry. Stick three green strips to the top of each strawberry in a star shape, using a little blob of glue. Using a large needle, make a hole in the top of the strawberry, in the centre of the star shape. Squeeze a blob of glue into the hole and insert a piece of florists' wire.

Fill the hole with glue and proceed to insert the base of the leaves into it, pushing the wire ends into the fruit.

Bananas

The bananas are made in a different way to the other fruit. Use the patterns below to create four cardboard shapes which are then taped together to make one banana.

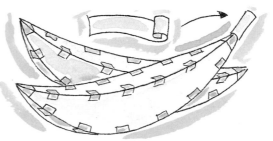

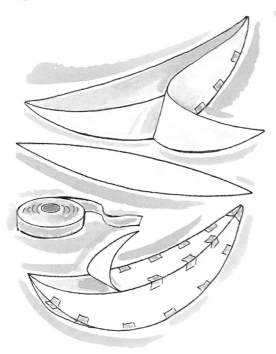

9 For each banana you need to trace off the shapes below and scale them up as described on page 17. Transfer these shapes on to the cardboard, then cut the shapes out. For each banana you will need two sides, one base and one top strip. Stick these together with masking tape, as shown.

10 To make the banana stalk, simply roll a long strip of paper coated in paste into a stalk shape, glue this to the end of the fruit and leave to dry. Proceed to make the required number of bananas, for example, three, and wrap each one in about three layers of smooth papier mâché strips. Leave to dry in a warm place and decorate as the other fruits, following step 6 and 7.

11 Once you are happy with the way you have decorated your fruit, you are ready to coat them with a glossy varnish.

Variations

This project explains how to replicate in papier mâché a number of different fruits of varying shape and colour. There is no reason why you cannot represent all types of fruit such as vibrant citrus fruits, a melon, peaches, apples and cherries using the same or similar methods shown in this project. You could also apply these techniques to make a selection of vegetables.

Note: *The spattering technique is an effective way to achieve a textured surface. Experiment with paint effects and highlighting the fruit, playing with different thicknesses and colours of paints.*

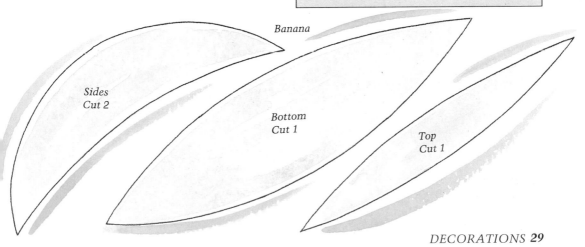

Banana

Sides
Cut 2

Bottom
Cut 1

Top
Cut 1

Christmas decorations

Cover card and twine with papier mâché to create a subtle and sophisticated range of Christmas decorations. These ornaments are finished in an interesting, distressed effect, which is easily achieved by painting and sanding different layers of colour. A little gold wax or paint gives a really festive finishing touch.

REQUIREMENTS
Mounting card
PVA glue
Twine
Flour and water paste
Newspaper strips
Fine grade sandpaper
White emulsion paint
Poster paints
Gold ink or wax gilt
Paper clips
Raffia or gold thread
Varnish

1 Using the shapes below as a guide, transfer a number of stars, hearts, circles and diamonds on to the card. Using a craft knife or scissors, cut out the shapes.

2 Cut the twine into 10 cm (4 in) lengths and glue these into a squiggle design on to the card shapes. Now proceed to cover the shapes with about three layers of papier mâché. Leave the shapes to dry.

3 When the shapes are thoroughly dry, smooth down the surface with the sandpaper. Apply a coat of white emulsion paint to the decorations and allow them to dry.

These Nordic-style Christmas decorations will add subtle colour and gentle highlights to your yuletide tree. They are quick to make and can be used year after year if carefully stored.

4 Using the coloured poster paints, paint each decoration in a different colour. Leave them to dry and then paint each decoration with a coat of white emulsion. Allow this to dry before applying yet another coat of paint, this time in a colour that will contrast with the first. For example, orange and turquoise, cream and green.

5 Once thoroughly dry, smooth down the surface of each decoration with sandpaper and you will notice the colours emerging from underneath.

6 Highlight the relief detail with gold; applying a little gilt wax or gold paint around the edges, too. Once dry, coat each decoration with matt or gloss varnish.

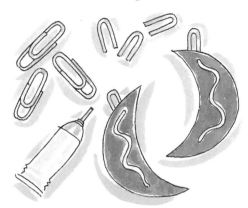

7 To make the hooks, cut some paper clips in half using wire cutters. Pierce two holes in the side of each decoration with a pin; add a blob of glue into each hole and insert the paper clip hook. Tie a length of coloured string, raffia or thread through each hook.

Variations

More glitz The decorations created in this project are very subtle and you may prefer something brighter. Make the ornaments in the same way but when you come to decorate them you could use glitter, sequins, spray paints and brighter colours.

Different shapes Why not experiment with alternative shapes, such as angels, bells, stockings, animals or snowmen?

Decorative egg cups

These ornamental egg cups are formed by taking papier mâché moulds directly from large size eggs. These shapes are then joined together and more papier mâché is added. The bold, colourful pattern and colour with which these egg cups are decorated, complements the simplicity of the shape.

REQUIREMENTS
Two large eggs
Needle
Petroleum jelly
Flour and water paste
Newspaper strips
All-purpose glue
Fine grade sandpaper
White matt emulsion paint
Poster paints
Varnish

1 First you must blow one or two eggs. To do this, pierce a hole in the top and bottom of the eggs using a needle. Hold the egg over a bowl or cup and blow into the top hole; the contents of the egg should emerge from the hole in the bottom.

2 Once you have blown one or two eggs (the more eggs you have for moulds, the quicker you will be able to make your egg cups), smother them with petroleum jelly.

3 Cover the larger half of the eggs with water-soaked strips of paper. Now apply two to three layers of papier mâché strips. Leave to dry in a warm place.

> **Note:** *Although we have suggested using petroleum jelly and a plain water layer of paper on the eggs, it is important that you avoid getting paste on the shell as the paste sticks very hard, preventing you from removing the eggshell when dry.*

Jolly, decorative eggcups make perfect containers for brightly-painted eggs. Vary the designs to match the decoration on the egg.

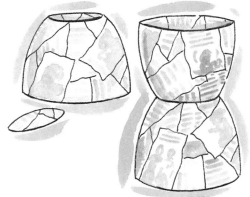

4 Once fully dry, ease the papier mâché shell from the egg. Particularly stubborn shapes may need to be slit with a craft knife to help remove them from the shell. If you do need to cut the shape, simply glue it back together again.

5 Once you have enough half egg shapes to make the number of egg cups you want (remember, you need two halves for each egg cup), trim the rough edges with scissors.

Take one of the pairs of half shells and, using the craft knife, cut a circle in the base, about 2.5 cm (1 in) in diameter. Now place the other shell half into this hole, applying glue at the point they meet to secure them. Now proceed to cover the egg cup shape all over in another layer of tiny papier mâché strips, neatening all the edges and joins. Leave them to dry in a warm place.

6 Once completely dry, gently sand the egg cups and apply a coat of white emulsion paint. When dry, decorate the egg cups with poster colours. Finish with a protective coat of gloss varnish.

Bull and cow

This vibrant, carnival-inspired, pair of creatures is built on basic wire mesh shapes which are then covered with papier mâché strips. Choose the smallest gauge chicken wire available when embarking on a wire-based project, you will be amazed what sort of detail can be achieved.

REQUIREMENTS
Small gauge chicken wire
Flour and water paste
Newspaper strips
Cardboard
Masking tape
Pins
Fine grade sandpaper
White matt emulsion paint
Poster paints
Twine
All-purpose glue
Varnish

1 Using a pair of old scissors or wirecutters, cut out the body parts from the chicken wire: a square measuring approximately 15 cm (6 in), a rectangle measuring approximately 7.5 x 5 cm (3 x 2 in) and four strips of wire for the limbs approximately 12.5 cm (5 in) long.

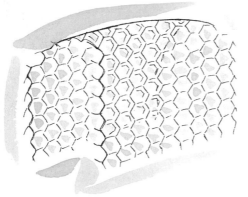

2 To make the main body, take the large square and bend it in half to form a narrow tunnel, tuck in the protruding bits of wire at each end, and along the bottom where the two edges meet.

Utterly appealing, this pair of little bovine creatures will capture the hearts of all onlookers. They make wonderful, personal gifts, though you might be reluctant to part with them, once they're made.

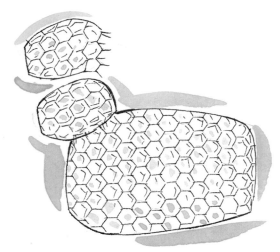

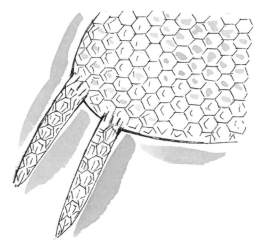

3 To make the head, take the smaller rectangle of wire and bend it also into a tube shape, tucking in the protruding bits of wire at one end (this is the nose) and use the blunt wire at the other end to attach the head to the body shape.

5 To attach the legs, simply bend the wire ends at the top around the wire of the body shape. They might be a little wobbly, but once you have applied the papier mâché they will become stronger. Do not worry about the lengths of the legs at this stage.

4 To form the legs, take the four strips of wire and tuck all the blunt bits of wire inwards, so you form a leg shape.

Note: When you are attaching the legs to the body of the bull, you may find a few strips of masking tape wrapped around the joins are of great help.
Rather than complete the papier mâché process over the whole bull shape in one step, you may find it easier to work on one leg at a time, allowing the paste and paper to dry between each one.

6 Apply three to four layers of papier mâché to the bull shape. It is important to wrap a number of long thin strips of paper and paste to the top of the legs where they join the body. This will ensure a secure joint. Keep the surface of the animal as smooth and lump free as possible by smoothing the papier mâché carefully with your fingers. Use long thin strips of paper around the legs. Leave the model in a warm place to dry.
7 Once completely dry, use the scissors or wirecutters to trim the legs so that the bull stands steady. Neaten the hooves by wrapping a few long strips of paper and paste around them.

Add the features in bright colours, remembering to paint a bold muzzle and forelock. The tail is simply a little twine, frayed at one end.

8 To make the ears, cut out two oval ear shapes from cardboard. Tape a pin to each ear and insert them into the head. Apply a few thin strips of paper and paste around the base of the ears. Leave the model once again in a warm place to dry.

9 Gently smooth down the surface of the animal with fine grade sandpaper. Apply a coat of white emulsion paint.

10 Choose a colour you wish to paint your bull. Apply the colour over the whole animal. Once dry, gently sand the surface lightly to break up the solid colour. Choose another colour that will show up on the base colour, and apply a blob on the head and on the chest.

11 Paint the hooves a dark colour. Use a finer brush to paint a stripe down the back bone of the bull in a contrasting colour. Spatter different colours on to the body, using bright colours that are likely to show against the body colour. Finally, using a fine brush, paint on the eyes in black and white.

12 To make the tail, cut a piece of twine roughly 10 cm (4 in) long. Fray the twine at one end. Paint the tail in a contrasting colour to the main body. Using the end of the paintbrush, pierce a hole at the end of the animal's body, fill with glue and slot the tail into position.

13 Once you are happy with your decorated model, apply a coat of matt or gloss varnish.

Variations

We have decorated our examples here in an abstract style. You may like to create a different finish. Possibilities could include a black and white, spotty or even a stripy bull.

Scale is another aspect of this project which you could vary; why not make a cow with two small calves?

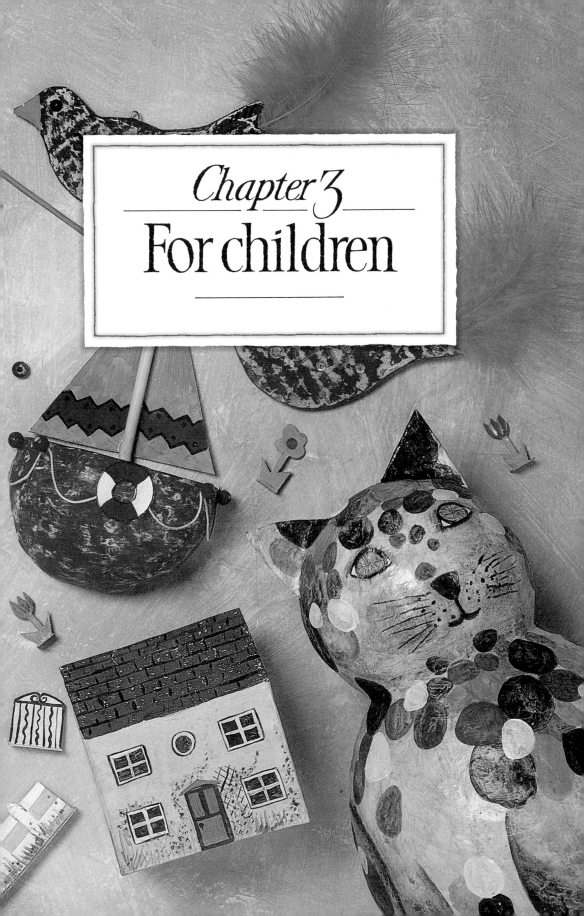

Chapter 3
For children

Sun mask

Because of their similarity to the shape of the head, balloons make an ideal mould for any papier mâché face or head decoration. Once you have made the basic face shape, the mask can be built up with more papier mâché or cut in a certain way to develop a particular character. Extra details in cardboard or twine can be added, and once the mask is finally decorated the result is sure to be stunning.

REQUIREMENTS
Balloon
Flour and water paste
Newspaper strips
Masking tape
Scrap paper
Cardboard
Fine grade sandpaper
White matt emulsion paint
Bright poster colours
Varnish
Thin elastic

1 Blow up a balloon and cover one side of it in two or three layers of papier mâché. Leave this to dry, but keep it away from any direct heat as the balloon will deflate.

2 Once the mask shell is dry, pop the balloon with a pin. The mask can now be built up – around the cheeks, nose, eyebrows etc – to form the face. Do this by screwing up small pieces of paper; tape them to the mask. Neaten these raised areas by layering papier mâché strips over them so they blend in with the rest of the mask. Add another two or three layers of papier mâché to the rest of the mask. Leave to dry.

3 Trim away the rough edge around the mask. Use a pencil to draw the eye sockets and the mouth. Cut these out using a craft knife. Now neaten all these raw edges using very small strips of paper and paste. Leave to dry once more.

4 To make the spikes around the top of the mask, lay it face up on to a piece of cardboard. Use a pencil to mark a curve around the top of the mask from where the spikes point. Draw about five or six spikes along the curve. Now cut this out.
5 Tape the curve of spikes to the top of the mask. Add a few strips of papier mâché to the join and leave in a warm place to dry.
6 Gently sand down the whole of the mask and apply a coat of white emulsion paint to both sides of the mask. Leave to dry.
7 Mark out your design on to the mask with pencil then paint the mask as you wish. Finish with a coat of varnish.

8 Once dry, use a large needle to pierce a hole in either side of the mask. Take a length of elastic and thread it through the holes, securing it with a knot on both sides.

This glowing sun mask makes a striking decoration for a child's room using bright, primary colours and a naive style of embellishment.

Boat wall plaques

A trio of wall plaques usually conjures up the image of three flying ducks, but we have taken that idea and introduced a completely different subject matter. Three balloons of varying sizes have been covered in papier mâché and combined with card, string and beads to create a trio of little boats. These colourful plaques make a refreshing alternative to the posters and pictures that usually clad a child's bedroom wall.

REQUIREMENTS
3 balloons
Flour and water paste
Newspaper strips
Thin cardboard
Masking tape
Fine grade sandpaper
White emulsion paint
All-purpose glue
Drinking straws
Poster paints
12 beads
String
Pair of compasses
Double-sided sticky pads

1 Blow up three balloons in different sizes. Cover the bottom half of each balloon with three or four layers of papier mâché strips, then leave them to dry in a warm place.

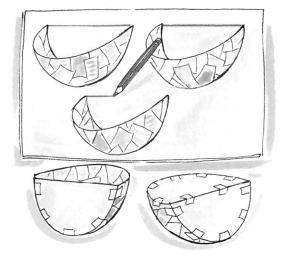

2 Pop the balloons and cut the three bowl shapes in half. Discard one half of each pair and trim the edges so that when you place the shape down on a flat surface, it lies neatly and does not wobble.

3 Place the three chosen boat hull shapes down on to a piece of cardboard. Draw an outline around the shapes. Cut these out and tape the pieces on to the back of the boats. To cover the tops of the boats, place the hull shapes upside down on to a piece of cardboard and draw around them. Cut these out and tape them into position.

4 Cover these hollow boat hulls in two or three more layers of papier mâché strips. Leave them to dry in a warm place.

5 Once dry, sand down the surface and apply a coat of white emulsion paint to the three boats. Leave to dry once more.

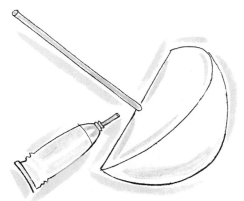

6 To make the masts, make a hole in the centre at the back of each boat hull using a craft knife. Place glue in each hole and insert a straw into each one, at different heights, according to the boat's size.

Create a flotilla of classic little sailing boats, using balloons as moulds, to adorn a child's bedroom wall.

7 To make the sails, cut three different-sized triangles from the card. Place glue along the back of the sails and attach them to the straws.

8 Apply a coat of white emulsion paint to the sails and masts. When the boats are dry, decorate them in a selection of poster colours. When the paint is completely dry, you might like to distress the paintwork on the hulls by rubbing them gently with the sandpaper.

9 Use a pair of compasses to draw three rubber ring shapes on to thin card. Cut these out and paint them in red and white.

10 Cut three lengths of string. Use the glue to stick the string, rings and beads to the top edge of the boats, as shown here.

11 Finally, coat each boat with gloss or matt varnish. Use the double-sided sticky pads to adhere the nautical trio to the wall.

Variations

Although we have chosen a nautical theme with bobbing boats, you could easily adapt this technique to come up with alternative ideas such as stylized animals, clown faces or flowers.

> **Note:** This project involves a lot of gluing, which can sometimes be fiddly; so keep your hands clean and ensure that between each such step you are patient and leave the glue to dry thoroughly. This will also strengthen the joins.

Exotic bird mobile

This attractive bird mobile illustrates one of the easiest techniques in papier mâché. Simple cardboard shapes are wrapped in strips of paper and paste. The bold decoration is achieved by layering vibrant colours and sanding them down, which is an ideal way of representing a subject as eye-catching as a flock of exotic birds. Sequins and feathers complete the models.

REQUIREMENTS
Corrugated cardboard
Flour and water paste
Newspaper strips
Fine grade sandpaper
White emulsion paint
Poster paints
Varnish
PVA glue
Sequins
Feathers
Paper clips
4 wooden batons or kebab sticks
Strong coloured thread

1 Using tracing paper, copy the bird template shown here and transfer this shape five times on to the corrugated cardboard. Cut out these five birds using a craft knife and cutting mat. Cover the bird shapes in two or three layers of papier mâché and leave them to dry in a warm place.

2 Gently sand down the rough surface before applying one coat of white emulsion paint to each bird on both sides. Allow the paint to dry.

3 Select a number of vibrant, strong and bright colours and apply these quite thickly, using a different colour for each side of each bird. Once completely dry, apply another coat of white emulsion paint. Once dry, apply another bright colour; choose a colour that will contrast well with the first colour that was applied, for example, purple on yellow, red on green, turquoise on pink.

4 When all the birds are fully dry, gently sand down and you will notice the colours beneath showing through, creating an interesting and very colourful effect.

5 With a fine paintbrush, paint a squiggle pattern on to each side of the birds, choosing a colour that will show up well. Paint the beaks in a clear yellow. When all the paint is dry, apply a coat of varnish on to each bird. Leave to dry.

6 Glue the sequins on to the sides of the birds and stick one on each side of the head to create the eyes. Use a needle to pierce a hole in the birds' tails, place a blob of glue in the hole and insert a feather.

> **Note:** *When you are ready to sand the surface to reveal the colours beneath, it is important that you use clean pieces of sandpaper for each side of each bird. If you continue to use the same piece, it will become smudged and the vibrant layering will not be so effective.*

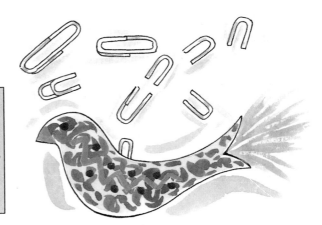

7 Cut three paper clips in half to make six loops (you will need five). Use a needle to pierce two holes 6 mm (¼ in) apart on the back of each bird. Dip the metal loop ends in glue and insert them into the holes.

8 Cut two batons or kebab sticks roughly 12–15 cm (5–6 in) long, and one baton approximately 23 cm (9 in) long. Paint a number of lengths of thread and tie a length to each bird, through the paper clip loop. Now tie a bird to the end of each shorter baton. Tie each one at a different length.

9 Using more thread, tie the batons with two birds to each end of the longer baton; tie them at different lengths. Finally attach the fifth bird to the middle of the long baton, so that it hangs above the other two batons. Tie a length of thread to the centre of the longer baton. Suspend your mobile from this last thread. Adjust the positioning of the birds and batons by sliding the knotted threads up and down.

Variations

We have decorated our mobile using sequins and a little paint detail; you might like to use other methods of decoration, such as glitter, metallic spray paints, or bright coloured beads.

Exquisite birds of paradise float in the breeze, their sequined plumage catching the light and their vivid tail feathers gently waving.

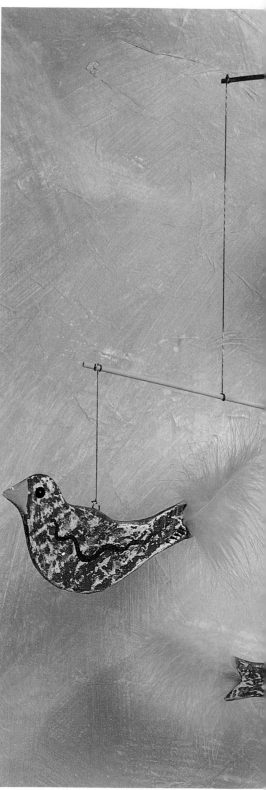

Fat cat money box

Money boxes have always been a popular subject to work in papier mâché, whether they are the classic rotund pig or a simple treasure chest. This project involves building up a rough cat body shape, using two papier mâché covered balloons, followed by a bit of building up here and there. Then you have the fun of creating a unique character with your paints.

REQUIREMENTS
2 balloons
Flour and water paste
Newspaper strips
All-purpose glue
Masking tape
Scrap paper
Thin cardboard
Wide brewer's cork
Fine grade sandpaper
White emulsion paint
Poster paints
Varnish

1 Blow up the two balloons, one bigger than the other (one will be the head and the other the body). Cover both balloons with two or three layers of papier mâché and leave in a warm place to dry. Do not place near direct heat as this will deflate the balloons.

2 Once fully dry, pop the balloons. Using the craft knife, slice a piece off the bottom of the smaller balloon and both the top and bottom from the larger balloon. Stick the head to the body, with glue or tape, and glue a piece of card to the base of the cat. Use masking tape to hold the glued areas together while they are drying, if necessary.

3 To build up the paws at the base of the cat and the cheeks on the face, simply screw up paste covered pieces of paper and stick them on to these areas. Neaten these built up areas by covering them with small strips of paper and paste.

4 To make the ears, cut out two triangles in thin card, and glue them on to the head, using strips of masking tape to hold them in place securely.
5 Proceed to cover the whole cat shape with two more layers of papier mâché so that all the built up areas and the ears blend in to create a successful cat shape. Leave the model to dry in a warm place.
6 Once completely dry, use the craft knife to cut a slit in the back of the head of the cat. In the base of the cat cut a hole the size of the cork. Now use sandpaper to smooth down the whole cat shape.
7 Apply one coat of matt white emulsion paint to the money box. When dry, lightly draw in the cat's markings, its nose and eyes before painting them. Slightly watered paints give more natural effect on the cat's body. Use the watery paints for shading around the paws and legs.
8 Once you are happy with the decoration, apply a coat of either matt or gloss varnish. Once the varnish is dry, insert the cork in the hole in the base of the cat.

This statuesque and handsome cat will keep your cash safely guarded. The basic shape is made up quite easily by moulding papier mâché over two balloons. Have fun decorating it; follow the design here, or make your cat resemble one you know, perhaps a black and white or tabby.

Note: When covering the balloons in papier mâché, you will find it a lot easier to use a large mug or a small bowl to support the balloons while working.

Miniature house and garden

This is an ideal project to make for and with children. Simply collect plenty of cereal boxes and other cardboard packets, and use them to build the house, hedges, kennel and greenhouse. Cover these in papier mâché and get carried away with the detail, painting in the flowers, vegetables and pond.

Our example is only a guide, make more buildings and other objects. Varnish helps to keep the model clean and protect it.

REQUIREMENTS
Thin cardboard (ie cereal packets)
Thick cardboard for base
Masking tape
All-purpose glue
Flour and water paste
Newspaper strips
White matt emulsion paint
Fine grade sandpaper
Poster paints
Varnish

1 Cut the thick cardboard so that it measures roughly 30 cm (12 in) square. Put to one side. Now trace the patterns shown here for the house, greenhouse, kennel, flowers and hedges. Enlarge and transfer these shapes on to the thinner card and cut them out. (Instructions appear on page 17.)

2 Make the house, greenhouse and kennel using masking tape to stick the card together and glue or tape the hedge shapes and flowers on to their little supports. Cover the base and the house, greenhouse and kennel in two or three layers of papier mâché. When complete, leave the pieces to dry in a warm place.

3 Sand down all the pieces before applying a coat of white emulsion. Also paint the hedges, fences and flowers. Leave them to dry.
4 With a light pencil, draw in details on the house, for example, the slates on the roof. Paint all the pieces with poster paints, using a fine paintbrush for the details.
5 For the base, follow the diagram to mark out the position of the path, vegetable patch and pond etc. Paint in these details. I sanded down the grass slightly to make it look more natural. The hedges are simply painted in various shades of green, then spattered with other lighter and darker colours to help them look three dimensional. (Details on paint techniques appear on pages 15 and 16.)

This project is tremendous fun, as you can add all sorts of bits and pieces once the base and main features have been created. Use up cereal boxes or other packaging for the cardboard.

Finish with gloss or matt varnish to all the pieces and the base on both sides. For extra protection give everything a second coat.

Variations
The basic principles used in this project could be employed using a different theme. You could make a farm, a garage, fire station, street of shops or park etc. You could also incorporate other miniature details such as animals and people.

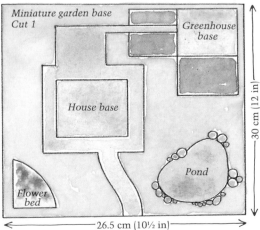

Miniature garden base
Cut 1

Greenhouse base

House base

Pond

Flower bed

30 cm (12 in)

26.5 cm (10½ in)

Left: the base, painted to show the pond, garden path, vegetable plot and flower bed. Below: the decorated house, kennel and a row of brightly coloured flowers. Coat the pieces with varnish so that they can be played with.

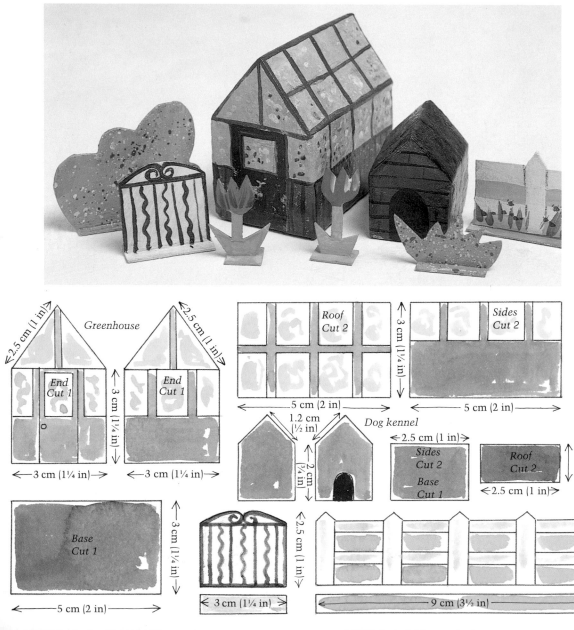

Greenhouse

2.5 cm (1 in) 2.5 cm (1 in)

End Cut 1 3 cm (1¼ in) End Cut 1

3 cm (1¼ in) 3 cm (1¼ in)

Roof Cut 2 3 cm (1¼ in) Sides Cut 2

5 cm (2 in) 5 cm (2 in)

1.2 cm (½ in) Dog kennel

2 cm (¾ in) 2.5 cm (1 in)

Sides Cut 2 Roof Cut 2 1.2 cm (½ in)

Base Cut 1 2.5 cm (1 in)

Base Cut 1 3 cm (1¼ in)

5 cm (2 in)

3 cm (1¼ in) 2.5 cm (1 in)

9 cm (3½ in)

9 cm (3½ in)

Roof
Cut 2

Back
Cut 1

9 cm (3½ in)

Front
Cut 1

House
base
Cut 1

9 cm (3½ in)

4.5 cm (1¾ in)

6.5 cm (2½ in)

Ends
Cut 2

6.5 cm (2½ in)

Base

Base

Base

Base

Base

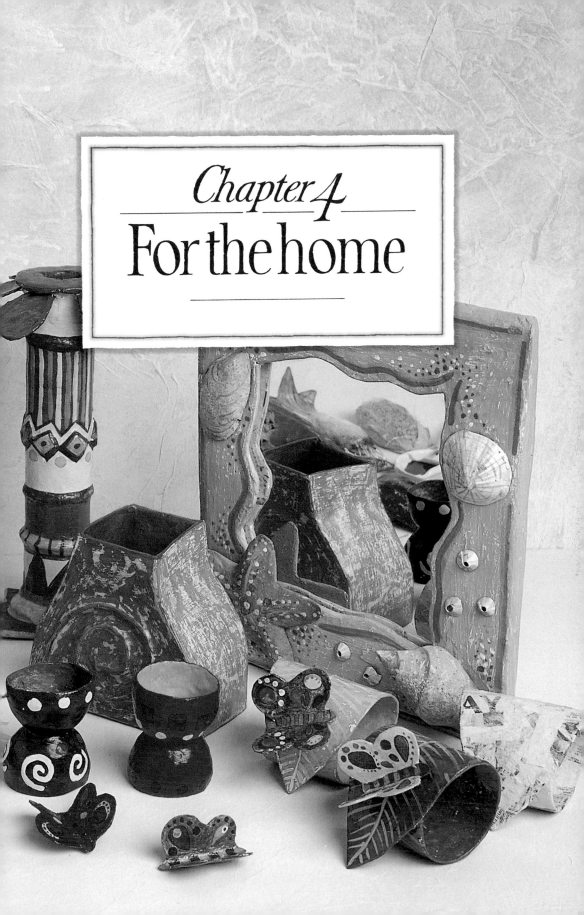

Chapter 4
For the home

Candlesticks

This project illustrates a great way of making use of the cardboard tubes found in the middle of kitchen paper towel rolls. Stick twine and string randomly up and down the tube, and build up with papier mâché strips. This basic idea can be decorated in any way you choose.

REQUIREMENTS
Cardboard tubes from paper towel rolls
String and twine
All-purpose glue
Thick and thin cardboard
Flour and water paste
Newspaper strips
Fine grade sandpaper
White matt emulsion paint
Poster paints
Varnish

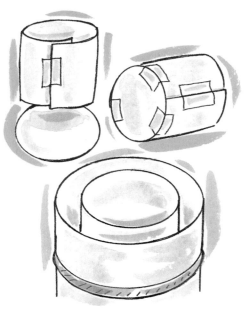

1 Wind lengths of twine and string at irregular intervals around the tubes, and stick them in place with glue. To create a variety of thicknesses, you can build up layers of string.

2 To make the base of the candlesticks, draw a bold shape, such as a star, or circle, on to thick cardboard. Cut out these shapes and glue them to the base of the tubes.

3 For the candlesticks to hold a candle, you must make a holder to sit inside the top of the tubes. Fill each tube with screwed up paper, leaving a gap roughly 4 cm (1½ in) from the top. Make up a smaller tube from cardboard, the diameter measuring a little larger than the average-size candle and the depth to correspond with the gap in the top of the candlestick. Cut a circle of card to cover the bottom of this smaller tube and stick it in place with glue. Insert the smaller tube into the larger one, gluing it in position. Repeat this for each candlestick.

4 To complete the basic structure, cut another piece of card in a flower, star or circle shape. Using a craft knife, carefully cut a hole in the centre of the shape, a little larger than that of an average-sized candle. Glue this to the top of the tube. Repeat this step for each candlestick.

5 Cover the candlesticks in two or three layers of papier mâché and leave them to dry in a warm place.

6 Gently sand down the surface of each candlestick then prime with a coat of white emulsion paint. Sand them down again before applying the poster colours of your choice. Finish with a coat of varnish for protection from wear and tear.

These stylish candlesticks are humble cardboard tubes, transformed with a little papier mâché, twine and paint. Make a matching pair, or have fun creating various designs.

Key cabinet

This delightful little folksy-style key cabinet is simply constructed from corrugated cardboard and masking tape. This basic structure is then covered inside and out with strip papier mâché. Once decorated, tiny hinges, screws and hooks are added to create a functional, practical and decorative item for the home.

REQUIREMENTS
Corrugated cardboard
Masking tape
Twine
All-purpose glue
Flour and water paste
Newspaper strips
Fine grade sandpaper
White matt emulsion paint
Poster paints
Varnish
Hinges
Latch
Cup hooks

1 Use the patterns shown overleaf for the basic cabinet shapes. Transfer these on to the corrugated cardboard, following the method described on page 17. Cut the shapes out on a cutting mat using a craft knife or scalpel and steel ruler.

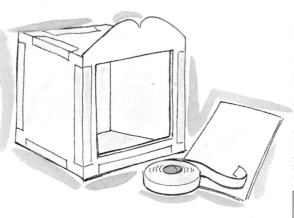

2 Join up the basic cabinet with masking tape. Glue two short lengths of twine in a curly design to the top of the cupboard as shown to provide relief detail.
3 Cover the cabinet inside and out, and the door, with papier mâché strips. Avoid lumps and bubbles by working slowly, smoothing the strips as you go. Leave the cabinet somewhere warm to dry.

4 When dry, gently sand the cabinet and door, then prime with one coat of white emulsion paint. Once again, leave the pieces to dry thoroughly.
5 Paint the cabinet and outside of the door in a colour of your choice using poster paints. When dry, sand gently for a slightly distressed effect. Paint the inside of the cabinet and door in a contrasting colour and pick out the relief detail and paint on a motif (a flower motif is shown overleaf for you to copy if you wish). Finish with a coat or two of matt varnish.

6 Once fully dry, attach the door and latch to the cabinet. Using a ruler, measure and mark where the hinges should fit on to the door. Make holes where the screws will go into the cupboard and door using a large needle. Add a blob of glue for extra strength. Gently screw the hinges into place with a small screwdriver, putting them on to the door first. The screws will probably come out on the other side, but don't worry about this, you can cover the ends with small pieces of papier mâché. Now attach the latch by screwing it into place.

Note: *When putting the screws, hinges and hooks into place, put a small blob of glue into the hole and on to the thread of the screw. This will make it that bit stronger.*

This pretty cabinet conjures up visions of Central Europe or perhaps New England. As well as being decorative in its own right, this charming little cupboard makes a handy tidy for your keys.

7 For the key holder, cut out two strips of corrugated card measuring approximately 15 x 2.5 cm (6 x 1 in). Glue them together and paint them. Once dry, glue this strip to the inside of the cupboard. When the glue is dry, screw in little cup hooks for the keys.

Variations
This little cupboard could be used for a number of different purposes. Incorporate a little shelf and use it for jewellery.

Paint the inside of the cabinet in a contrasting colour to the outside. Add a number of little cup hooks on to the cardboard strip inside to hold your keys.

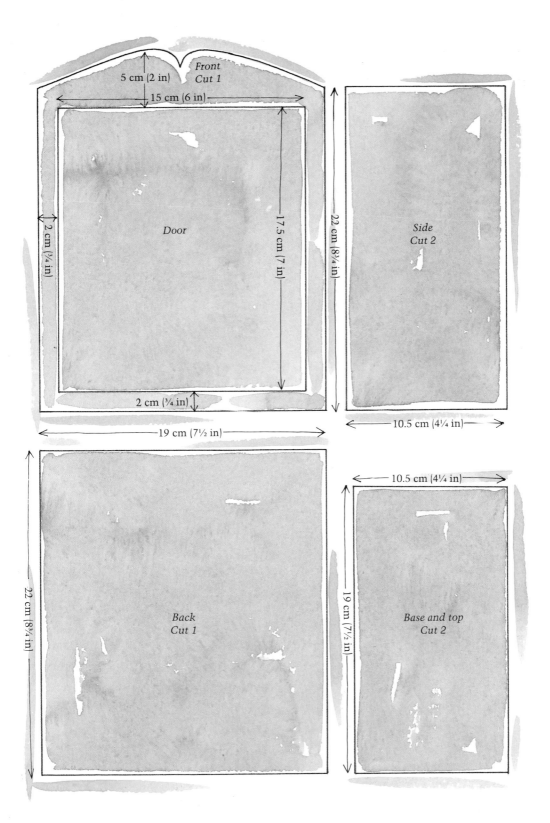

Front
Cut 1

5 cm (2 in)

15 cm (6 in)

Door

2 cm (¾ in)

17.5 cm (7 in)

2 cm (¾ in)

22 cm (8¾ in)

Side
Cut 2

10.5 cm (4¼ in)

19 cm (7½ in)

22 cm (8¾ in)

Back
Cut 1

10.5 cm (4¼ in)

19 cm (7½ in)

Base and top
Cut 2

Grecian vase

This stylish vase combines classical and modern elements to create a quirky and eye-catching design. It is made from a balloon mould using papier mâché strips with wire to support the handles and spherical feet for ornamental detail. The surface of the vase provides an opportunity to experiment with abstract designs and you might like to refer to a book or magazine for ideas. As it's not watertight, the vase can only be used to display dried, silk or paper flowers or decorative grasses.

REQUIREMENTS
Pear-shaped balloon
Flour and water paste
Newspaper strips
Scrap paper
Wire
All-purpose glue
Pins
Fine grade sandpaper
White matt emulsion paint
Poster paints
Varnish

1 Blow up the balloon into the shape of a light bulb. Cover the surface completely with two or three layers of papier mâché. Leave it to dry in a warm place but away from direct heat.
2 When completely dry, pop the balloon and trim the edge at the thinner end, or neck, with scissors. Cover the vase with another two layers of papier mâché, smoothing it down with your fingers to avoid lumps and air bubbles. Fold strips of paper over the 'lip' to enhance and strengthen the edge. Leave the vase in a warm place to dry thoroughly.
3 For the feet, tightly roll a ball of scrap paper in your hand and cover it with strips of papier mâché. When the desired shape has been achieved put it in a warm place to dry. You will need to cover the growing ball with papier mâché and allow to dry thoroughly three more times.

Note: Before you embark on decorating your vase, you may find it helpful to draw the design lightly on to the surface first. Use art books, magazines and pieces of pottery to inspire you in your decoration.

4 To make the handles, push a length of wire into the side of the vase, bend it into the desired handle shape and secure it by pushing the free end of wire back through the vase. Bend the wire ends back inside the vase so that they are flush with the inside surface. Apply a number of strips of papier mâché to these wire handles. To strengthen the fixing points, it is also necessary to apply papier mâché to the inside joins.

5 To attach the feet, push a pin through the bottom of the vase, from the inside out. Using a dab of glue, push the ball 'foot' on to the pin and leave the glue to dry. Repeat this process for the other three feet. To make neat joins, add papier mâché strips around the feet and base.
6 When completely dry, gently sand down the entire surface. Apply a base coat of white emulsion paint, reaching as deep into the vase as possible. Leave the paint to dry.
7 Decorate the vase in a range of patterns using a selection of colours and brushes. When you are happy with the design, finish with a coat of matt or gloss varnish.

A contemporary interpretation of a classical style, this striking vase is made using a number of techniques.

Seashell mirror

This seashore-inspired mirror is a simple cardboard frame covered in strip papier mâché. Delicate shells have been created by taking moulds from a number of real shells. These, along with cardboard barnacles and a papier mâché starfish, are arranged in an attractive composition on to the basic frame resulting in an appealing addition to a bathroom or bedroom.

REQUIREMENTS
Mirror tile
Corrugated cardboard
Flour and water paste
Newspaper strips
All-purpose glue
Shells for moulds
Petroleum jelly
Thin card
White matt emulsion paint
Poster paints
Fine grade sandpaper
Varnish

1 Using a ruler, measure and mark on to the corrugated cardboard two squares, approximately 6 mm (¼ in) larger all round than the mirror tile. On one of the squares, draw a window to create a frame approximately 5–6 cm (2–2½ in) wide all round. Cut out these two pieces carefully with a craft knife.

2 Stick the mirror tile in the centre of the cardboard square and set aside. Cover the frame with two layers of papier mâché, both back and front, taking care to coat the inside edge of the window. Place this under a book or heavy weight and leave it to dry. (This will prevent the frame from buckling.)
3 Aligning the edges carefully, glue the papier mâchéd frame on to the cardboard/mirror base. Apply another two layers of papier mâché, covering the back of the mirror and all the joins and edges. Leave this to dry thoroughly.

4 In the meantime, cover a selection of shells with petroleum jelly. Apply one layer of paper strips soaked only in water, then add the papier mâché strips, building up two or three layers. Leave these in a warm place to dry thoroughly.
5 Remove the paper shells from the moulds. With some, you may need to cut them using a sharp craft knife. Keep the cut as clean as possible and then glue the two halves together neatly.

> **Note:** *When taking moulds from the existing shells, it is important you choose suitable shells. Avoid shells with lumpy, porous surfaces, try using mussels, clams and cockles.*

Shells and starfish adorn an attractive bathroom mirror. You could use these sea creatures to decorate other items: boxes, picture frames, bowls or even turn them into jewellery.

6 To make the starfish, draw and cut out a star shape from thin card. Screw up pieces of pasted paper and build up the textured surface of the starfish. Cover the whole starfish shape with strips of paper and paste. Leave to dry.

7 To make the barnacles, cut small circles from thin card, snip into the middle of the circles and overlap the edges, securing them with glue. When you have made enough of these, paint them with white emulsion paint, then colour them in cream or beige. Leave to one side.

8 Now choose the colours you wish to paint the shells and starfish. Paint these using techniques such as distressing and spattering. (Paint techniques are discussed fully on pages 15 and 16.) Put these aside.

9 Sand the whole of the mirror frame and apply one coat of white emulsion paint. Rub down the surface once more and apply a base coat of poster paint. Once dry, rub the paint gently with the sandpaper once more.

10 Arrange the shells, starfish and barnacles on the frame and secure them with glue. Once dry, add tiny painted details if you wish, before finishing with a coat of matt or gloss varnish.

Variations

For really stylish and sophisticated decoration, why not paint your seashore mirror in a monochromatic scheme? Try greys and silver, bronze and gold or shades of blue, finishing with a little metallic dusting powder for extra lustre.

Gilded bowl

A bowl is probably one of the easiest projects to tackle when using papier mâché. Most people are likely to have attempted one at some point, probably as children in the art room.

There are a number of decisions to make before embarking on this project: the shape of the basic mould, how thick you want to make the bowl, and how you are going to decorate it. The simplicity of the shape makes a bowl an ideal base upon which to experiment with all kinds of pattern, collage and paints, as well as building up relief detail or adding handles or feet.

You can papier mâché on either the inside or outside of the bowl mould; although using the outside is probably easier.

REQUIREMENTS
Bowl for mould
Petroleum jelly
Newspaper strips
Flour and water paste
Fine grade sandpaper
White matt emulsion paint
Poster paints
Gilt wax
Varnish

1 Cover the surface of the bowl with a layer of petroleum jelly. Wrap the bowl in newspaper strips soaked only in water; this will prevent the papier mâché sticking to the mould. Apply approximately three layers of papier mâché strips to the bowl and place it somewhere warm to dry.

2 Once the bowl is dry, remove it from the mould. It should simply fall away, otherwise prise it off using a blunt knife. At this stage, you may like to apply a few more layers of papier mâché, or you may like to keep it thin and fine as the one here. The rim has been gently torn to create a jagged edge.

3 When you are happy with the thickness of the bowl, and the edge has been torn, you can proceed to gently sand down the surface of the bowl on both sides. Apply a coat of white emulsion paint, both inside and out. Repeat this step, so that the bowl is primed.

4 Now paint the bowl in the colour of your choice and leave it to dry. You might like to gently sand the painted surface to create a grainy effect. Rub gilt wax on to the rim of the bowl and over the surface. Finally, coat with matt or gloss varnish for protection.

A simple bowl painted in deep cobalt blue has been lightly rubbed with gilt wax to pick out the natural texture of the papier mâché. The bowl's wavy rim has also been given the Midas touch.

> **Note:** When choosing a bowl mould, select one that is sturdy and non-porous, for example, fired ceramic, metal, glass or plastic. Avoid wood or anything with a lumpy surface.

Variations

You can make a bowl to almost any scale providing you have a suitable mould. Don't be frightened of working large; even a big bowl will be quite sturdy once dry and varnished. Also try different decoration techniques; instead of simply painting, apply a background coat of paint, then incorporate leaves, coloured embroidery threads, coloured tissue papers etc before varnishing. Or add these in between the papier mâché layers.

Butterfly napkin rings

This very simple project uses strip papier mâché and cardboard decorated with brightly coloured poster paints. The end result is fun, eye-catching and totally practical. These could be decorated to make an original and special addition to the table at a barbecue, party or seasonal event like Christmas or Thanksgiving.

REQUIREMENTS
Thin cardboard
All-purpose glue
Masking tape
Flour and water paste
Newspaper strips
Fine grade sandpaper
White matt emulsion paint
Poster paints
Varnish

1 Use the template provided to draw the napkin ring shape on to thin cardboard. Draw at least four rings, then cut these out.

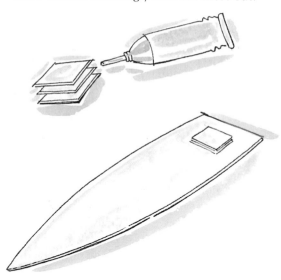

2 Cut out a number of 6 mm (¼ in) squares of card. Glue three of these together and stick them 12 mm (½ in) from the blunt end of the napkin ring shape. Repeat this process on the other strips. Now bend the pointed end round so it overlaps the blunt end and covers the block of card. It should overlap by roughly 4 cm (1½ in). Glue to the block of card, securing the join with masking tape until it is fully dry. Repeat steps 2 and 3 with the other rings. Bend the pointed leaf end upwards slightly.

3 Cover the rings in three or four layers of papier mâché, keeping the edges neat and smooth. Once complete, leave them to dry in a warm place.
4 Sand the rings inside and out before applying one coat of white emulsion paint. Put to one side.

5 To make the butterflies, use the template provided as a guide and transfer the shapes on to thin card. Cut the shapes out and, with the back of a craft knife, score a line down the middle of each butterfly's body. Bend into a butterfly shape. Apply one layer of papier mâché to each butterfly and leave it to dry. Once dry, smooth down with sandpaper and coat with white emulsion paint.
6 Decorate the napkin rings and butterflies with poster paints. Use a detailing brush for the butterflies as their markings are quite fiddly. Apply veins on the leaves in either a lighter or darker green than the base colour.
7 Mount the butterflies on to the top of the rings, securing them with glue. Finish with a coat of varnish.

Variations
The overlap cardboard technique shown in this project is an ideal method to use when making papier mâché napkin rings. You may like to decorate them in a different way, possibly using papier mâché holly at Christmas or tiny parcels for a birthday.

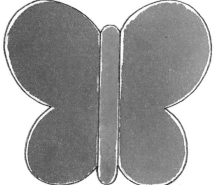

These novel napkin rings have been made to resemble leaves, each one bearing a visiting butterfly. Make them the same, or vary each butterfly's decoration, as those here.

Left: template of the butterfly shape, to trace. Below: napkin ring wrap-around. This will need enlarging to twice this size, as described on page 17.

Fridge magnets

This realistic set of vegetable fridge magnets is created by building up simple cardboard shapes with pieces of bunched-up paper and strip papier mâché. To recreate those distinctive details that successfully illustrate each vegetable, we have incorporated other materials, such as crêpe paper and string.

REQUIREMENTS
Cardboard
Flour and water paste
Newspaper strips
Fine grade sandpaper
White matt emulsion paint
Poster paints
String and fine rope
All-purpose glue
Green crêpe paper
Varnish
Magnets

1 Each vegetable shape is first drawn on to cardboard. Enlarge the shapes shown below or draw your own shapes freehand on to the cardboard. Cut each shape out. (Information on transferring patterns appears on page 17.) Note that the leek has an extra leaf which is cut as a separate piece.

2 Each vegetable is created by bunching up the papier mâché strips and moulding them on to the cardboard shapes. When you have formed the basic shape, neaten them by smoothing over strips of paper and paste. For **broccoli**: build up the head with paper lumps but apply only strips of paper and paste to the stalk. Do not neaten the broccoli head with papier mâché strips to create a realistic finish. For the **leek**: using masking tape, add the extra leaf and bend it forwards before covering it in papier mâché strips. Leave all the pieces to dry thoroughly in a warm place.

3 Sand down all the vegetables and then apply a coat of white emulsion paint. Leave to dry thoroughly.

4 Paint each vegetable in a base colour, for example, shades of green and yellow for the corn and broccoli, orange for the carrot. When dry, gently sand the painted surface in places to break up the colour. Now, using a fine paintbrush, paint in the details.

A medley of realistic vegetable fridge magnets make wonderful note holders. Each vegetable is made using the same basic method.

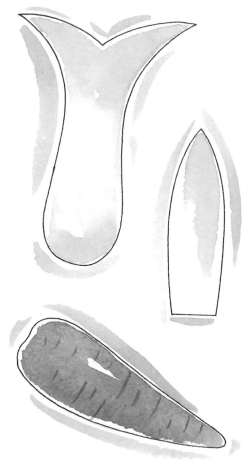

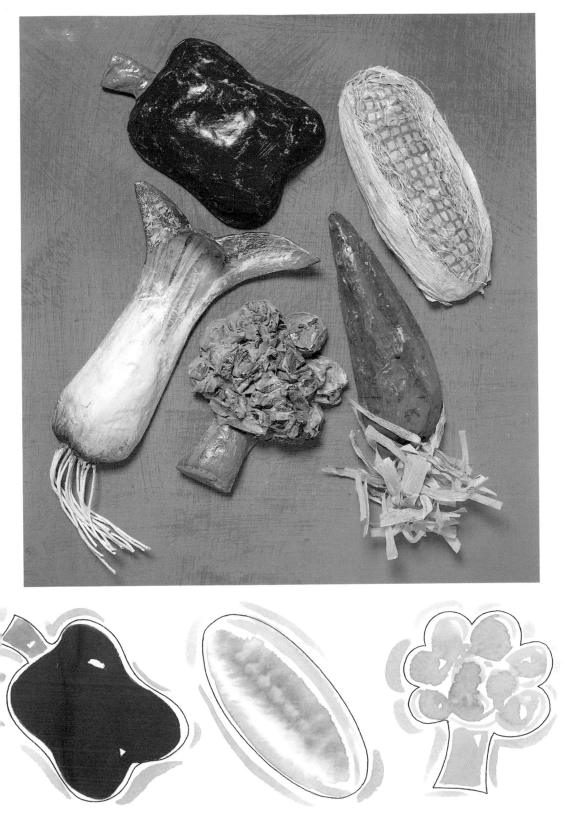

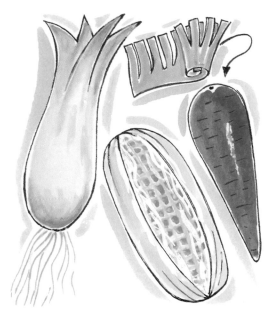

Pen holders

Gather scraps of cardboard and cardboard tubes to make these colourful pots which form great containers for keeping those stray pens, pencils and paintbrushes in one place. Glue twine, or small pieces of cardboard to the basic shape, and then cover it in layers of papier mâché to achieve delicate relief detail. This detail can be highlighted at the decorating stage to make a really attractive piece, perfect for any desk or study.

Use the tubes from kitchen paper towel rolls and cardboard from cereal boxes.

REQUIREMENTS
Cardboard tubes
Cardboard scraps
Masking tape
String
All-purpose glue
Flour and water paste
Newspaper strips
Fine grade sandpaper
White matt emulsion paint
Poster paint
Varnish

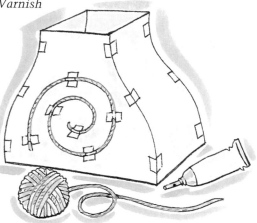

5 For the final touches, you will need to add bits of string or crêpe paper. For the **leek**: add the stringy roots by making a number of holes in the base with a thick needle. Squeeze glue into each hole and then push a length of string into each hole. Add a little brown paint to the strings and the base of the leek to resemble earth. For the **carrot**: cut the carrot top from green crêpe paper. Make a hole in the top of the carrot using a knitting needle, squeeze glue into the hole and insert the crêpe paper. For the **corn**: tease apart a piece of fine rope so it resembles the stringy parts of a corn cob. Glue these along each side of the corn. Add a few pieces of green crêpe paper for authenticity.
6 Finish each vegetable with a coat of varnish and, when dry, glue a magnet to the back of each one.

Variations

Try different vegetables or fruits: radishes, tomatoes, cauliflower, onions, mushrooms, bananas, pineapples or strawberries are all good shapes to emulate.

Note: Try to keep the papier mâché lumps from becoming too wet when building up the vegetable shapes, otherwise the finished shape could look bulky, wrinkly and unconvincing.

1 Begin by making up the pen holder shape. Use pieces of cardboard and/or cardboard tubes; join the pieces together with masking tape. Add relief details by sticking small pieces of cardboard – corrugated works well – or pieces of string to the surface.
2 Proceed to apply two or three layers of papier mâché smoothly to the pen holder. Try to avoid lumps or air bubbles. If it is not too awkward, papier mâché the inside of the pot as well. Leave in a warm place to dry.
3 Sand down the surface and apply a coat of white emulsion paint. Leave to dry. Once completely dry sand the surface down again.

Practical and decorative pen holders made from cardboard scraps, tape and papier mâché. They can be decorated in almost any style you wish.

4 Using your poster paints, mix up colours you wish to paint your pots. Choose a theme or simply apply the colours in an abstract way. We have shown a number of different examples.
5 When you are happy with your design and it is fully dry, apply a coat of gloss or matt varnish for protection.

Variations
We have illustrated three quite different ways to decorate the pots. There are endless alternatives; here are a few ideas: letters and numbers, figures, animals or flowers.

> **Note:** *When you are making up the basic shape of your pen holder, it is a good idea to make the base a little larger, as this will prevent the pens and pencils from tipping the pots over.*

An alternative design and colourway, this pencil holder is painted in brown and off-white, with a Greek-style border in relief.

Lamp base

We have used a balloon to achieve the shape of this papier mâché lamp base. Small cardboard tube legs have been added and parts of the balloon have been removed to create a simple rotund shape which has then been decorated with layers of pretty, coloured tissue papers.

The decoration on this lamp base is a collage of tissue paper shapes, each one overlapping to create an interesting array of translucent colours.

REQUIREMENTS
Balloon
Flour and water paste
Newspaper strips
Thin card
Masking tape
All-purpose and PVA glue
Fine grade sandpaper
White matt emulsion paint
Poster paints
Coloured tissue papers
Varnish
Light fittings

1 Blow up the balloon to the required size and shaped like an egg. Cover it with about three layers of papier mâché. Leave the piece somewhere warm to dry, but not in direct heat, as this will deflate the balloon. When completely dry, burst the balloon.

2 To make the legs, cut out three pieces of thin card measuring roughly 8 x 10 cm (3 x 4 in); although don't worry about the exact length of the legs at this stage as they will be trimmed later. Roll the card into tubes, securing the join with tape. Fix each tube to the base of the balloon shape, keeping them equidistant and sticking them in place with glue and tape. Trim the bottom of each leg to ensure the base stands firm.

3 Using the craft knife, take a clean slice off the top of the balloon; the angle of the slice should be parallel to the surface on which the balloon is standing. The diameter of the circle cut away should be 10–13 cm (4–5 in).

4 Cut a circle of card to fit over the hole you have just made. Stick the card into position using masking tape. Now cover the whole lamp base in a few more layers of papier mâché. Leave it in a warm place to dry thoroughly.

5 When completely dry, gently sand down the surface of the lamp base. Prime the lamp with white emulsion paint. Once dry, smooth it down again.

6 Coat the whole lamp base in a base colour and leave it to dry. Gently sand the painted surface to break up the flat, opaque colour just a little.

7 Cut up a number of 'blob' shapes from the coloured tissue papers in a variety of sizes. Prepare a solution of water and PVA glue and use this to adhere the tissue shapes in an irregular pattern to the lamp base. Overlap the shapes for an interesting effect. Leave the glue to dry before finishing with a coat of varnish.

8 Finally, you must fit the electrical components into the lamp base. Use a craft knife to make a small hole at the base of the lamp, behind one of the legs. Use the knife to cut a larger hole in the flat top of the lamp; this is to hold the bulb socket into position, so you will probably need to draw around it to get an accurate measurement.

9 Feed the plugless cable down through the top hole and out through the bottom hole. You can then attach the plug in the usual way. Place a little glue around the edge of the hole in the top of the lamp, and fit the light socket into position. Once dry, the lampshade and bulb can be fitted and your lamp is complete.

Chapter 5
Special gifts

Colourful platter

Big, bold, hand-painted crockery is very fashionable and popular. This platter is a more economical, yet nonetheless, equally delightful papier mâché version. And, it is one of the most basic and uncomplicated projects to undertake.

Because the platter is large, it lends itself to exotic decoration. Take your ideas from books or magazines and transfer or adapt the designs you see on to the platter.

The final piece could be exhibited on a mantel, suspended from a wall, or used on a table centre to hold fruit.

REQUIREMENTS
Large flat dish for mould
Petroleum jelly
Newspaper strips
Flour and water paste
Fine grade sandpaper
White matt emulsion paint
Scrap paper
Poster paints
Varnish

1 Choose a suitable mould to create the platter. A large flat dish or tray is ideal. Apply the petroleum jelly to one side of the dish or tray. (You can work on either side of the dish.)

2 First, apply a layer of paper strips which have been dipped in water only; this prevents the papier mâché sticking to the mould. Proceed to apply three layers of papier mâché strips, overlapping the edge of the mould as you work. Avoid air bubbles and lumps and try to keep the layering as even as possible. Leave it to dry.

3 When completely dry, gently ease the platter from the mould. Trim the edge using scissors. Now apply two or three more layers of papier mâché to the platter, neatening the edge by folding thin strips of paper and paste all the way around. Neaten the underneath of the platter also. Leave to dry in a warm place.

4 Sand down the edges and surface on both sides before applying a coat of white emulsion paint. Leave the platter to dry, then smooth it down once more and apply another coat of paint.

5 On scrap paper, draw a rough sketch of your chosen design before transferring it on to the platter with a pencil. Paint the design with poster colours. When the paint is completely dry, finish with a coat or two of matt or gloss varnish.

Variations

Choose a theme, and make a number of platters in various sizes. Try traditional pottery designs, such as old Wedgwood, Shelley or Clarice Cliff. Art deco designs work particularly well on papier mâché as they are usually simple and bold. Books on the history of pottery and ceramics, or antique guides, should give you plenty of ideas to consider.

This delightful ornamental platter displays a wonderful 1930s-style design. Even if your freehand painting is good, it is worth first mapping out your design on paper before transferring it – in fine pencil – to the platter.

Hawaiian doll

Although this is one of the more ambitious projects, the result is well worth the patience required when manipulating the wire pieces into the body parts. The limbs and body section are all made up and painted separately and then joined together using a large needle and strong thread. Completing the doll's charm is the addition of a cute little raffia skirt and strings of brightly coloured beads.

REQUIREMENTS
Small gauge chicken wire
Flower and water paste
Newspaper strips
Fine grade sandpaper
White matt emulsion paint
Poster paints
Varnish
Large, upholsterer's needle
Strong button thread
Coloured raffia
Scrap of ribbon or fabric
Needle and thread
Popper studs
Small beads

1 Using old scissors or wirecutters, snip the chicken wire into suitable size pieces to make the body parts. You will need two rectangles measuring approximately 15 x 10 cm (6 x 4 in) for the arms; two rectangles 20 x 10 cm (8 x 4 in) for the legs; a piece measuring about 25 x 20 cm (10 x 8 in) for the body and another piece about 18 cm (7 in) square for the head. (The head will be joined on to the body before the papier mâché is applied.)

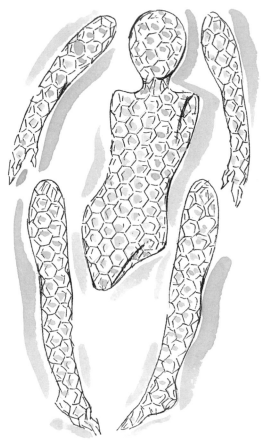

2 Manipulate the pieces of wire into the required shapes. This process may take some time to achieve accurate shapes, but persevere and try to keep the shapes as rounded and neat as possible. Remember to make feet and hand shapes at the end of the limbs. Fix the head to the body by intertwining the ends of the wire.

Papier mâché is the perfect medium for this primitive and naive model. The body, head and limbs are fashioned in chicken wire before being built up with strip papier mâché.

through the top of the side of the body, bringing it out on the other side of the body. Now push the needle into the other arm, as shown. Pull the thread fairly tight and secure it with a large knot. Repeat this process for the legs.

3 Cover all the pieces in three to four layers of papier mâché. Leave them to dry in a warm place, then sand them down thoroughly before coating each shape with white emulsion paint.
4 Using suitable size paintbrushes and a range of brightly coloured poster paints, paint the skin, hair, facial features, bodice and shoes, etc. When the paint is dry, varnish each piece.

6 To make the skirt, cut lengths of raffia about 13 cm (5 in) long, stitch these to a length of ribbon. Sew popper studs at each end to fasten it around the waist. To make the jewellery, thread small coloured beads on to thread and knot the ends together.

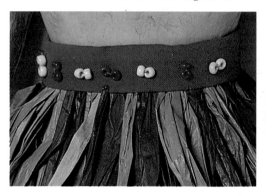

The waistband is made from ribbon. Stitch strands of raffia on to the ribbon with thread.

5 To join the body parts together, take a very long upholsterer's needle, attach a length of strong thread or string and knot the end. Insert the needle into the side of the top of one of the arms and bring it out the other side. Then pierce the needle

> **Note:** *When layering the paper strips on to the body pieces, you can always build up areas such as thighs, kneecaps, ankles, thumbs and elbows by adding lumps of papier mâché and then smoothing them over with more strips.*

Carriage clock

This grand carriage-style clock is built up from a simple cardboard structure made using the patterns supplied as a guide. A number of papier mâché techniques are incorporated in this project, including using string to build up relief detail, creating columns from kitchen paper towel tubes and forming spheres from bunched-up paper. A small clock mechanism and hands are simply attached to the structure to complete an attractive and functional piece which anyone would be delighted to display on a mantel or shelf.

Use either mounting board or a sturdy corrugated cardboard. The little clock mechanisms can be purchased from craft shops or specialist suppliers, see page 92 for more details.

REQUIREMENTS
Cardboard
Masking tape
Paper towel tube
PVA glue
String
Flour and water paste
Newspaper strips
Scrap paper
Pins
Fine grade sandpaper
White matt emulsion paint
Poster paints
Gold paint or gilt wax
Varnish
Clock mechanism and hands

In keeping with its classical style, this stylish clock is painted in cream and gold.

1 First, make up the structure from cardboard. Use the patterns shown here as a guide, and cut out the card on a cutting mat, using a craft knife and steel ruler.

2 Using masking tape, assemble the cardboard to form the basic clock shape. To make the columns, cut the paper towel tube in half lengthways and glue the two pieces on to either side of the clock front. Glue the two clock face circles together, then stick them to the middle of the clock.

3 Make relief patterns by gluing lengths of string in lines down the length of each column and also in two squiggles on the triangle at the top of the clock. Leave to dry.
4 Cover the clock shape neatly with papier mâché. Apply about three layers, using smaller strips when working on the relief detail. Once you have covered the whole clock adequately, leave it to dry.
5 Now make up about 12 balls the size of large grapes out of papier mâché. The easiest way to do this is to screw up a piece of paper the size of an envelope into a small ball, then cover it in thin strips of paper and paste, rolling the ball shape in the palms of your hands until it is round and smooth. Leave the balls in a warm place to dry.

6 Sand down all the papier mâché surfaces; this may take a bit of time, but persevere and get right into the crevices. Once you have completed the sanding, use glue to stick the balls into place. Use the pins to help keep them secure. Allow the glue to dry.
7 Paint the clock in white emulsion paint and leave to dry. Rub down the surface briefly once more and proceed to apply another coat of paint.
8 Now choose a colour you wish to paint your clock. We chose cream and brown with gold highlights. Apply the paint and allow to dry before adding the relief detail in gold.
9 For the clock numbers, use a light pencil to draw them first, then a fine paintbrush to apply the paint. When you are happy with the result, coat the whole clock in varnish. You might like to give the clock two coats of varnish. Allow each coat to dry before applying the next.
10 Finally, insert the clock mechanism following the manufacturer's instructions. You will need to cut a hole in the clock face the size of the shaft of the mechanism to do this. If the mechanism is not tight enough against the inside of the clock, pad it out with little pieces of card. Now attach the hands, putting the small one on first.

Variations
To simplify this project, use a small sturdy box as your basic shape, adding on the relief details and columns as described above.

Note: *If you are not confident enough to draw the numbers on the clock face freehand, why not trace numbers from a book or use some rub down numbers sold in sheets from stationery shops.*

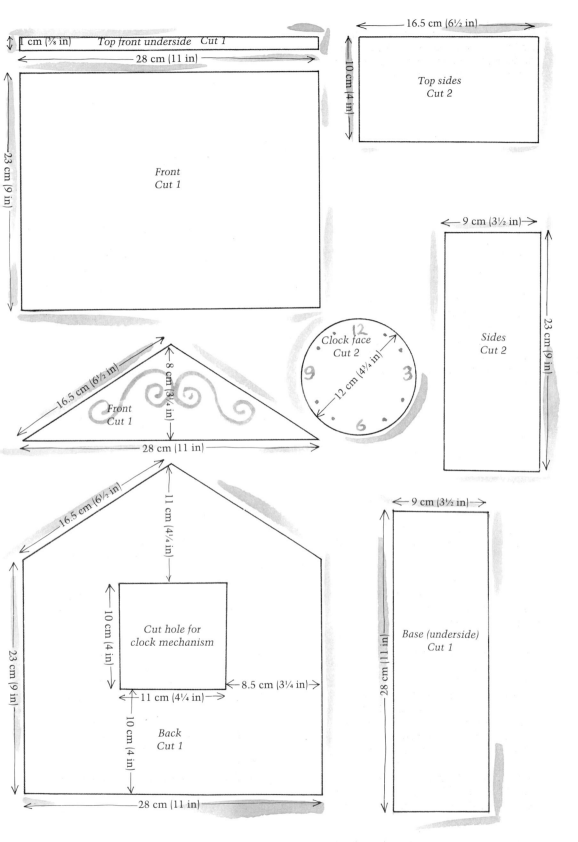

1 cm (⅜ in) Top front underside Cut 1

28 cm (11 in)

23 cm (9 in)

Front
Cut 1

16.5 cm (6½ in)

10 cm (4 in)

Top sides
Cut 2

9 cm (3½ in)

Sides
Cut 2

23 cm (9 in)

16.5 cm (6½ in)

8 cm (3¼ in)

Front
Cut 1

28 cm (11 in)

Clock face
Cut 2

12 cm (4¾ in)

11 cm (4¼ in)

16.5 cm (6½ in)

10 cm (4 in)

Cut hole for
clock mechanism

8.5 cm (3¼ in)

11 cm (4¼ in)

10 cm (4 in)

Back
Cut 1

23 cm (9 in)

28 cm (11 in)

9 cm (3½ in)

Base (underside)
Cut 1

28 cm (11 in)

Paper pulp jewellery

Small strips of paper have been mashed to a pulp and then moulded into balls of different sizes. (Full details on how to make papier mâché pulp appear on page 14.) The rough texture that occurs through this process makes an interesting surface to decorate with layers of paint and metallic dust which, in turn, makes a subtle finishing touch.

The various size beads can be combined with attractive coloured cord, clasps or other jewellery findings to make original and stunning accessories.

REQUIREMENTS
Papier mâché pulp
Large, sharp needle
White matt emulsion paint
Poster paints
Metallic dust or powder paint
Varnish
Coloured bead cord
Necklace clasp
Earring wires or studs
Strong, all-purpose glue

1 To make the beads, take a handful of the pulp, squeeze out as much of the water as you can and form it into a ball shape. Continue to make a number of these in different sizes. Place them on a tray and leave in a warm place to dry.

2 Once the balls are all dry, make a hole in each one by piercing the needle through the middle of them. You may need to twist the needle to help it break through the dry pulp.

3 Coat each bead with white emulsion paint and leave them to dry. Choose which colours you would like to decorate your beads. Mix up the colours and apply the paint with a brush or sponge. You may like to add a number of layers, to achieve an interesting effect. You could also spatter the paint on to the beads (see page 16).

4 Once you are happy with your beads, apply a small amount of metallic dust to them. You can do this by applying it lightly with a dry brush or painting it on mixed with water.

5 When you are happy with the colour scheme and the beads are dry, apply a light coat of gloss or matt varnish.

6 Cut the cord to the required length. Attach the clasp to one end, string on the beads, then add the clasp at the other end. You may need to use pliers to help you close the jewellery findings. The earrings are made by threading the beads on to wires or by gluing them on to blank studs.

Variations

The beads we have featured in this project are classically shaped but you could mould the paper pulp into a variety of other shapes, for example cubes, tubes or ovals. Also, you could thread the beads together with others made from different materials: metal, wood or even plastic would all complement the papier mâché perfectly.

Another fun concept is to squash the paper pulp into tiny chocolate moulds. Coat the insides of the moulds with petroleum jelly and compact the pulp in. When dry, tap out the shapes to use on brooch findings.

> *Note: When painting the beads and applying the varnish you may find it helpful to thread the beads on to a piece of wire or a skewer or something similar to hold them still.*
>
> *When you are deciding how to position the beads on to the cord, experiment with a variety of alternative arrangements before you settle for a set design.*

Paper pulp beads can be turned into any type of jewellery: necklaces, bracelets or earrings. Dust the beads with metallic powder or gilt wax for a finishing touch.

Pot pourri box

Cardboard is an excellent base on which to apply papier mâché. When made up into the basic box and lid, paper strips and paste are applied in even layers over the whole surface. Various details are then added, such as the papier mâché spheres and once sanded and primed, the box is ready for decoration.

The box featured in this project has been designed with small holes in the lid to allow the scent of the pot pourri within to disperse into the room.

REQUIREMENTS
A3 piece of mounting board
Masking tape
Flour and water paste
Newspaper strips
Fine grade sandpaper
PVA glue
White matt emulsion paint
*A selection of paintbrushes, including one
    for details*
Poster or gouache paints
Gloss or matt polyurethane varnish

1 Using the pattern overleaf as a guide, draw the box and lid pattern on to the mounting board with a pencil and ruler. Place the board on to a cutting mat and carefully cut out the pattern using a sharp craft knife and metal ruler. Cut out the holes in the lid with the tip of the craft knife.

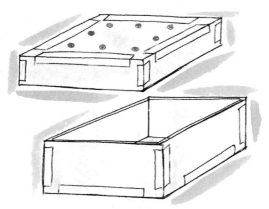

2 Fold the box and lid into shape, stick the sides together with strips of masking tape.
3 Mix together the flour and water paste until it resembles thick batter (see page 15). Tear up the newspaper into small strips and squares and put these into the paste.

4 Proceed to cover the box and lid with the pasted paper strips, both inside and out. Take care not to cover the holes in the lid. Apply just one layer for now and put the pieces to one side.

5 To make the spheres which serve as the legs and knob, take a piece of newspaper, approximately 15 cm (6 in) square, soak it in paste and screw it up tightly into a ball. Continue to cover it with strips of soaked newspaper, keeping the shape as neat as possible, until the sphere measures about 2.5 cm (1 in) in diameter. Repeat this step to make four other spheres. Leave them to dry in a warm place.

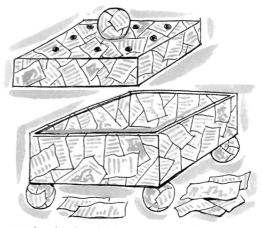

6 Take the dry spheres and smooth them down with sandpaper. Using the PVA glue, stick one sphere to each corner of the box and stick one on to the middle of the lid. To secure these spheres more firmly in place, tear up long, thin strips of newspaper, soak them in paste, and wrap them around the spheres and the corners of the box.

The delicate fragrance of a favourite pot pourri is released through the small holes in the lid of this attractive papier mâché box.

Little ball feet are made from scrunched up and soaked paper which are covered in thin strips of papier mâché. Sand them well when dry.

7 Cover the box and lid with two more layers of pasted strips, then leave the pieces to dry in a warm place.

8 Take the dry box and lid and smooth them down with sandpaper, both inside and out. Apply one coat of emulsion paint, let this dry and sand lightly again. Paint on the top coat and once dry give a buffing with sandpaper to provide an interesting surface on which to work.

9 Using a fine pencil, draw the violet pattern on to the box. Trace the violets shown here if you are not confident to draw your own flower freehand.
10 Using a fine paintbrush, paint the violets and leaves in appropriate colours with poster or gouache paints. Paint the spheres in one colour – dark green to match the leaves – works well.
11 Once the decorated box is complete, apply a coat of varnish to the box and lid, both inside and out. Allow to dry and apply a second coat for a really durable finish.

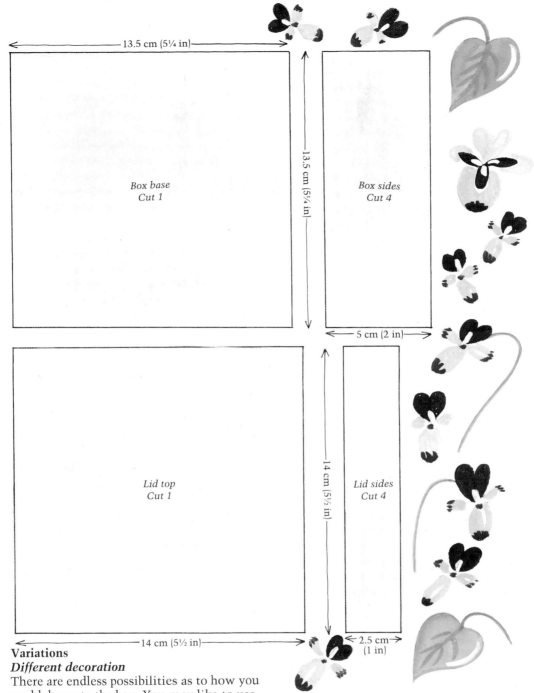

├─────── 13.5 cm (5¼ in) ───────┤

Box base
Cut 1

13.5 cm (5¼ in)

Box sides
Cut 4

├← 5 cm (2 in) →┤

Lid top
Cut 1

14 cm (5½ in)

Lid sides
Cut 4

├─────── 14 cm (5½ in) ───────┤   ├← 2.5 cm →┤
(1 in)

Variations

Different decoration

There are endless possibilities as to how you
could decorate the box. You may like to use
an animal or figurative theme to inspire the
decoration, or possibly simple abstract
patterns using bright and bold colours and
markings.

Little boxes

Try making several boxes of different sizes.
These can be decorated similarly and
grouped together to hold jewellery,
stationery or sweets.

*Note: When attaching the spheres to the
box, you may find it helpful to pierce a
long dress pin through the sphere into the
point of the box where it is to be attached.
Although the glue will stick the sphere to
the box, the pin will hold it in place that
little more firmly.*

Further reading

Inspiration for decoration can be gathered from a huge variety of sources. Try magazines, books on design, folk art, African, South American and Latin American art books.

Bawden, Juliet. *The Art & Craft of Papier Mâché*. Mitchell Beazley, 1990.
Haines, Susanne. *Papier Mâché*. Letts, an imprint of New Holland, 1990.
Owen, Cheryl. *The Creative Book of Paper Crafts*. Salamander Books, 1990.

Useful addresses

Many of the projects in this book require very simple materials, such as newspaper and flour, which can be found in most homes. Decorative finishes, such as paints and gilt wax, are readily available from any art supplier or good stationery store. Varnish can be purchased from DIY or hardware stores.

United Kingdom
Craft Supplies Ltd
The Mill
Millers Dale
Nr Buxton
Derbyshire SK17 8SN
(*suppliers of clock mechanisms*)

Paperchase
213 Tottenham Court Road
London W1A 4US
Tel: 0171 580 8496

T N Lawrence & Son Ltd
117–119 Clerkenwell Road
London
EC1 5BY
Tel: 0171 242 3534

W H Smith
(Head office)
Greenbridge Road
Swindon SN2 3LD
Tel: 01796 616161
(*branches throughout the country*)

Arjo Wiggins Fine Papers Ltd
130 Long Acre
London WC2E 9AL
Tel: 0171 379 6850

Winsor and Newton
Whitefriars Avenue
Harrow HA3 5RH
Tel: 0181 424 3200
and
51 Rathbone Place
London W1P 1AB
Tel: 0171 636 4231

Australia
Artwise
13 Wilson Street
Newtown
NSW 2042
Tel: (02) 519 8234

Wills Quills
164 Victoria Avenue
Chatswood
NSW 2067
Tel: (02) 411 2627

The Paper Merchant
316 Rokeby Road
Subiaco
WA 6008
Tel: (09) 381 6489

Oxford Art Supplies
221 Oxford Street
Darlinghurst
NSW 2010
Tel: (02) 360 4066

New Zealand
Faze Papers
32 Alfred Street
Onehunga
Tel: (09) 622 2220

BJ Ball Papers
395 Church Street
Penrose
Tel: (09) 579 0059

Rosehill Paper Supplies
Bremmer Road
Drury
Tel: (09) 294 7506

The Paper House
7 Carmont Place
Mt Wellington
Tel: (09) 276 2683

Bostick NZ Ltd
78 Leonard Street
Penrose
Tel: (09) 579 9263

Index